Why Do Flies Eat Doggy Poop?

Why Do Flies Eat Doggy Poop?
and other poems

by L. W. Lewis

with original drawings by Charles Clary

Red Pumpkin Press

P.O. Box 40

Rutledge, Tennessee 37861

ISBN: 0-9711572-0-0

LCCN: 2001091155

second edition

For my children

Jill

Julie

Samantha

Their lives inspired me to write.
I love them more than I love two Teddy Bears
and an arachnid.

WEBSITE UNDER CONSTRUCTION
If you wish to purchase a signed copy
or to contact the author directly, L. W. Lewis
my be reached at the email address:

Redpumpkinpress@aol.com

Contents

The Not Too Funny Section

Special thanks to Gwynne Fisher for final editing

Why Do Flies Eat Doggy Poop?

My Doggy Has No Tail

My doggy has no tail,
That's what people say.
But he doesn't need a tail,
To go outside and play.

It's true he has no tail.
Not even a little bit.
But what dog needs a tail,
Just to run and play and sit.

And if he has no tail,
Why should I even care?
He's such a special doggy,
With lots of love to share.

How do I know he loves me?
That crazy little mutt.
True, he can't wag his tail,
But he sure can wag his butt.

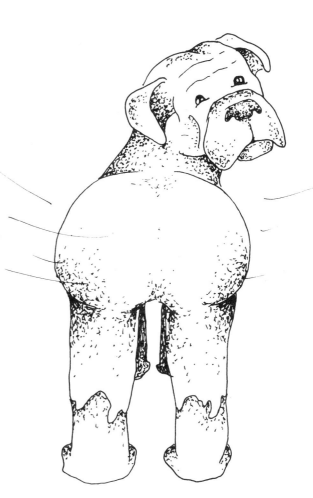

My Barbie

I got a brand new Barbie,
And she is truly great.
I call her Skater Barbie
When she twirls a figure eight

She can go in water.
She's nice and trim and slim.
I call her Swimmer Barbie
When I take her for a swim.

She has pretty dresses.
She likes to skip and prance.
I call her Barbie Dancer,
Because she loves to dance.

But my brother played with matches.
And by the time that he was through,
I had to change my dolly's name,
Now I call her "Barbie-Que."

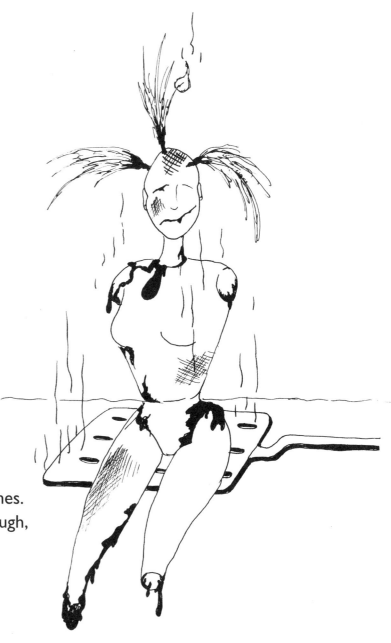

Christmas

I woke up very happy
Because today's the twenty-fifth.
I ran into the living room
To open up my gifts.

But there weren't any presents
And no Christmas tree at all!
Where was my Nintendo game
And my new basketball?

I woke up both my parents,
But they just laughed at me.
They didn't seem to care
That we had no Christmas tree.

When I get older, they'll be sorry
I'll remember this awful day,
And how my parents treated me
On the twenty-fifth of May!

Why Do Flies Eat Doggy Poop?

Why do flies eat doggy poop?
Don't they want an ice cream scoop?
If I were a fly, I wouldn't even try it.
I'd say to other flies, "I'm on a diet".

And how does one eat with grace or style,
Something that lies in a big smelly pile?
If doggy poop was the last meal you had
I know for sure your breath will smell bad.

Flies like poop. I don't know why.
I'd rather eat an apple pie
Poop is disgusting; it's stinky and bad.
Yet, it's the best meal a fly ever had.

There are lots of things I would love to be
Like a dog, or a horse, or a fish in the sea.
But never, ever, wonder why
I would not want to be a fly.

5

Etiquette

Etiquette is how to eat.
Which knife to use when cutting meat.
There are many rules in etiquette books.
But it's a lot simpler than it looks.

Never shove noodles up your nose.
Don't wrap spaghetti between your toes.
Never eat soup with a knife and fork.
Don't put mud on beef or pork.

Mashed potatoes don't go on your head.
Never eat chicken if it's not dead.
You don't eat dinner standing up.
Don't blow bubbles in your cup.

Go to restaurants wearing clothes.
Never use a napkin to blow your nose.
Close your mouth each time you chew.
Don't let gravy spill on you.

I did not become this well bred,
From anything I studied or read.
Just common sense was all it took.
I've never read an etiquette book.

Tommy

Tommy is two years older than me.
He's already five, and I'm just three.
But I don't think that Tommy's too smart.
When kindergarten opened, he didn't start.

First off, Tommy didn't learn the alphabet,
And Tommy can't really speak well yet.
But we watch television every day.
Then Tommy and I go outside and play.

For three full years our friendship's grown.
He's always with me. I'm never alone.
Nobody else could ever take his place,
Especially, when he wags his tail, or licks my face.

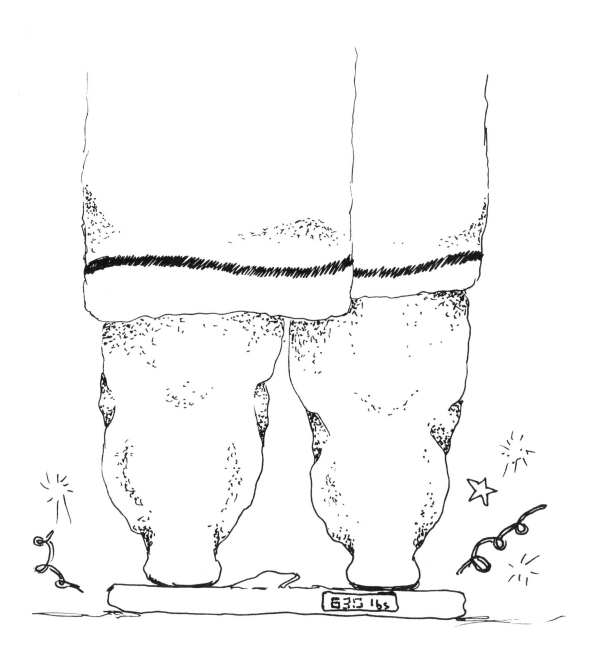

My Weight

I wouldn't say I'm fat.
I don't weigh that much.
Maybe a little heavy,
But only just a touch.

There are lots of other things
That weigh much more than me,
A walrus and an elephant,
A polar bear and redwood tree.

Compared to all those other things
My weight is lighter than it sounds.
I got on the scale yesterday,
I'm just six-hundred thirty pounds.

The Guppy

My brother got a dog.
I just got some fish.
So I put a guppy
In the puppy's water dish.

But the puppy didn't like that.
He bit off the guppy's head.
Now my brother is responsible
That my favorite fish is dead.

So I offered him a trade.
As fair as he could wish.
That tiny new born puppy,
For both pieces of my fish.

But my brother wouldn't do it.
He even tried to spoil it.
He took my favorite little fish,
And flushed him down the toilet.

Dog Food

I fed my brother dog food,
My mother is really mad.
But it's the very best dog food
My little brother ever had.

She screamed and called the doctor.
Her eyes are filled with tears.
I guess I shouldn't tell her,
He's been eating it for years!

A Bicycle Made From Balloons

If I had a bicycle made from balloons
I could pedal right up to Jupiter's moons.
While I was working my way to the stars
I could find out if there is life on Mars.

I could collect such wonderful things
Like rocks from Neptune or Saturn's rings.
Maybe I would catch some shooting stars
They could be headlights on my handlebars.

Or I could find out just how it feels
To fly with comets as bicycle wheels.
But Mommy fears a black hole or worse,
And she won't let me leave our universe.

13

Easter

Some kids believe in the Easter Rat.
But me, I would never believe in that.

And others believe in the Easter Goat,
But chances of that are quite remote.

I've heard tell about an Easter Snake,
But I'm pretty sure that story's a fake.

And this I find a really big surprise,
There are kids who believe in Easter Flies.

I would never believe, of course,
Like those who say there's an Easter Horse.

No, as for me (and you may think it funny)
Well, I believe in the Easter Bunny.

15

My Daddy's Head Is Broken

My daddy's head is broken,
Right on the very top.
He used to have hair grow there,
But something made it stop!

My Mommy plucks her eyebrows.
Could she have plucked his head?
Did she sneak into the bedroom,
While he was sleeping in his bed?

At the beach last summer,
I remember he had hair.
I'll bet when he was swimming,
Some fishy bit him there?

I've really been quite worried,
About my daddy's head.
So I asked my mommy,
And this is what she said.

"Your daddy has no sickness,
That isn't what it's called.
He's just getting older,
Your daddy's going bald."

My Mommy's Not So Small

My mommy's not so small.
She's seven feet in all.
She puts shoes on two,
And she's five of them tall.

And seven feet, I think,
Is taller than a camel.
So with just another seven feet,
She'd be the world's tallest mammal.

Or maybe she'd need
seven and a half
To make her taller
than a grown giraffe.
But my mommy
is not small.
In fact,
    she's really
        very tall.

College

If it's about going to college,
I've made my final decision.
I'm not going to Harvard
Because they do long division.

They don't even use a number,
They divide by a number square.
So I'm not going to Harvard
If they make me do that there.

I'm already taking English,
I'm learning how to spell.
And every day in pre-school
I do Play-Doh really well.

But if they make me do long division,
There is a good chance that I would fail.
So I'm not going to Harvard.
I'll probably go to Yale!

19

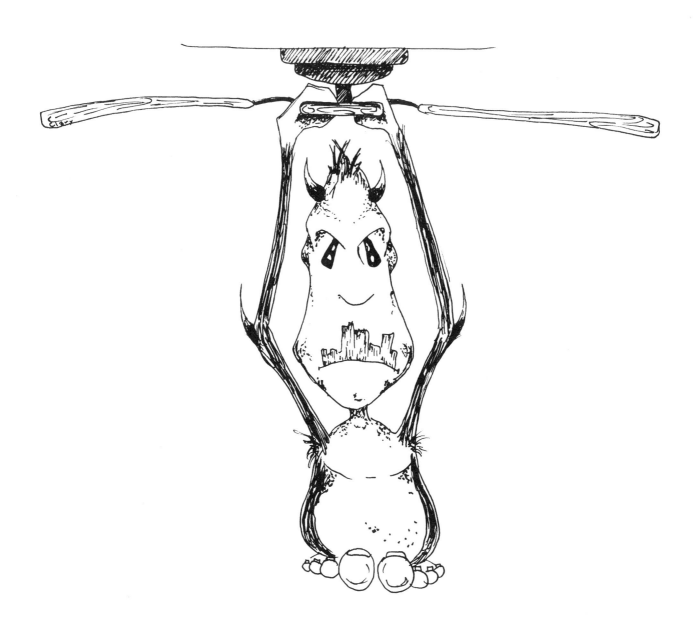

20

The Monster Under My Bed

My parents didn't listen to what I said
I know there's no monster under the bed.
Do you think I'd believe such silly things,
Like monsters under my mattress springs?

I'm not afraid like some little boys
All you'll find are a few of my toys
There's a puzzle, a ball, a Jack-in-the-Box,
And don't be surprised if you find dirty socks.

I'm a big boy, so don't think for one minute,
My room is dark and I'm afraid to be in it.
I never cry or scream, like my little sister.
(But since she got her own room, I sure have missed her.)

I'm very brave. I'm not afraid of the night.
But do you suppose you could leave on the light.
He's not under my bed, but I have this strange feeling,
The monster is hiding—up there on the ceiling.

The Color Red

My daddy screams at stoplights.
He must hate the color red.
We've stopped at quite a few of them,
You should hear the things he's said.

I have never seen him so crazy,
And he's never been so mean.
It's just the red that bothers him,
He seems fine with yellow and green.

I still like the color red,
I think it's really cute.
It's the color of Rudolph's nose,
And the color of Santa's suit.

Daddy used to like the color red.
He bought me this hat, this dress, and shoes.
But red is now the color
That gives my daddy the blues.

Kids shouldn't make their daddy mad.
That's just the way it goes.
So by the time we get to Grandma's,
I won't be wearing clothes.

My Bicycle

I built myself a bicycle,
The wheels turned out square.
You may think it would bother me,
But really, I don't care.

It makes lots of noise when you ride it,
The front wheel really thumps.
But the road can be awfully rocky,
And you don't even notice the bumps

24

The Bath

When I get older, and I have a daughter,
I won't bathe her in toilet water.
It might be tempting if I get rushed,
But one mistake, and she could get flushed.

Since I'm not really sure where the water goes,
At changing time, I'd have to flush her clothes.
Many things down there wouldn't taste that great
So if she wanted to eat, she'd have to wait.

I wonder how could I rock her to sleep?
I could jiggle the handle if she's not too deep.
But how could she go outside in the summer?
Just to kiss her I'd need to call a plumber.

So I'll never treat my daughter that way.
I'll take really good care of her every day.
She'll eat good food and I'll buy her nice clothes,
And if I'm rushed, I'll bathe her with a hose.

Grandpa

My grandpa's getting on in years.
He even has hair inside his ears.
He's kind of bent and walks real slow,
But he takes me to the movie show.

He doesn't throw a ball too well.
But he always has a story to tell.
Sometimes, when I feel blue,
He'll read to me, a book or two.

When things get tough, and I get sore,
He'll take me to the ice cream store.
We lick our cones while we sit and chat,
I'm glad I have a grandfather like that.

His skin is wrinkled.
     There's no hair on his head,
So that's where I kiss him
     when he tucks me in bed.
And he always smiles
     and tells me I'm smart.
Then he winks and says
     that I live in his heart.

Yesterday I heard my mommy say,
"It won't be long, and he'll pass away."
I hope he won't pass away too long,
I really miss him, every time he's gone.

Walter The Fish

Walter was a little fish.
Who lived in a little brook.
But no one ever caught him.
He'd leave the bait and eat the hook.

Kitty Litter

My brother is eating kitty litter!
I tried some too, but it's really bitter.
But Bobby says that it's my fault,
I'd like it better, if I used more salt.

So I added salt and took a bite,
But still, the flavor wasn't right.
There were other things we tried to do.
Mustard and catsup to name a few.

But I'm not eating more tonight,
I just can't get the recipe right
I'll try again some other day,
But I'll wait until the cat's away!

The Fiddle

My hands are way too little,
So it's hard to play a fiddle.
And the music isn't right,
The strings are way too tight.

There is no way at all
That I can play this song.
Not if I use this fiddle,
The bow is way too long.

Yet I'm suppose to be dainty,
Mommy says to be proper and prim.
How does she expect me to do that,
With a fiddle stuck under my chin!

But soon my hands will be bigger,
My fingers will be long and thin.
Then I can give up this fiddle,
Mommy says I can play violin.

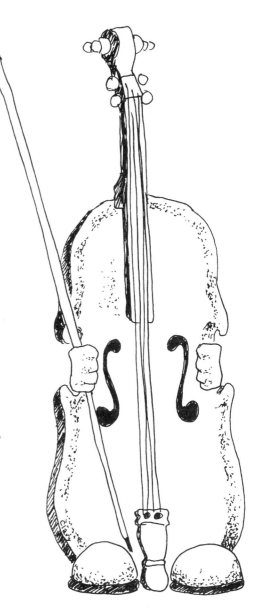

29

I Hate To Lose

I like to win
But I hate to lose.
I scream a lot
And throw my shoes.

I haven't lost in quite awhile,
Not because I've improved my style.
I haven't lost to a he or she,
Because no one wants play with me.

30

Cheating

I will not do what some other kids do,
I will not lie or cheat.
I'll never do what those kids do,
Even if it means defeat.

Because if I win by cheating,
I will always know inside,
That I really did not beat you,
Only that I cheated or lied.

And if, by chance, you beat me,
I can look you straight in the eye.
Perhaps you can say, 'You beat me'.
But you can't say, 'I did not try'.

There is no shame in losing,
Not if you've done your best.
If your were in the game each minute,
If you never stopped to rest.

Just play as well as you can,
Always be fair and true.
Cheating can't prove how good you are,
So you'll only be cheating you.

Bathing Kitty

I bathed our kitten and she's squeaky clean.
But now she's afraid of the washing machine.
She's crying and meowing. I think it's stress.
I used gentle cycle, and permanent press.

At first she swam, but a little later,
She got too close to the agitator.
I tried to grab her. She was out of reach.
All I could do was add more bleach.

Cats hate soapy water so it's hard to win.
But mine wasn't happy with rinse or spin.
So I took her out early when she started to cry.
I thought she'd feel better if she could tumble dry.

How else do you keep an animal clean?
I love my kitten. I don't want to be mean.
I'm sure I made a big mistake.
I shouldn't have washed her with my snake.

A Boy In Church

I saw a boy in church today,
He had on the nicest clothes.
Who would have been quite handsome,
But his finger was in his nose.

Don't ever pick your nose in church,
It's not a polite thing to do.
Your finger might get stuck up there,
And people will stare at you.

I never pick my nose in church.
I never act strange or queer.
I sit there very quietly.
And I just pick my ear.

My Sister's Sister

My sister's sister is beautiful,
She wears such pretty clothes.
And she is very popular,
With everyone she knows.

My sister's sister is fabulous.
She has beautiful eyes and hair.
She's never conceited or snotty.
And she's always willing to share.

My sister's sister is wonderful,
She is kind and gentle and sweet.
She is the kind of little girl
I know you'd love to meet.

I adore my sister's sister.
And the reason happens to be,
That I'm my sister's sister,
My sister's sister is ME!

Fishing

My daddy took me fishing,
But he won't take me anymore.
He said till I get older,
I'll stay with Mommy on the shore.

He says the bait stays in the bucket,
That you don't throw it in the lake.
And fishies don't eat sandwiches,
Or your mommy's chocolate cake.

You never throw a fishy back,
Just to try and save his life.
And don't cut Daddy's fishing line
When he lets you hold a knife.

You are quiet when you're fishing
You don't jump, or scream, or shout.
But the thing that made him maddest,
Was when I caught that eight-pound trout!

The Horsefly

My daddy told a lie.
He said he saw a horse fly.

A horse can't fly,
You can bet on that.

They don't have wings,
And they're much too fat.

What if one pooped
Way up in the sky?

If it fell on you,
Then you might die.

So I think my daddy lied.

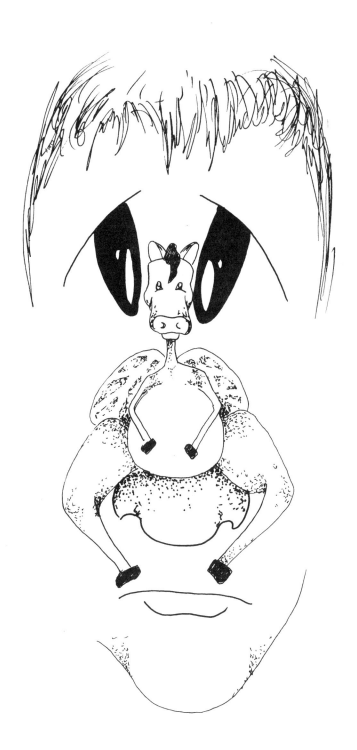

On Picking A Pet

I wouldn't want to have
A spider for a pet.
Spiders are as scary
As anything can get.

And frogs are slimy,
They wiggle and they're icky.
And if you let one kiss you,
Its tongue is really sticky.

It sure doesn't take a wizard
To know you wouldn't want a lizard.
They have way too many scales,
And their bodies are mostly tails.

But those are my only choices,
I have to pick one or the other.
So I guess my parents are right.
We're keeping my newborn brother.

My Sticky Dolly

My dolly's kind of sticky,
I fed her bread and jam.
But my dolly doesn't smell bad,
Because she wouldn't eat the ham.

I call my dolly Sissy,
Her dress is powder blue.
In the middle of her forehead,
I drew a pink tattoo.

Both her shoes are missing,
But to find them won't be hard.
One is at a neighbor's house,
The others in our yard.

I truly love my dolly,
I would never do her harm.
It was just an accident,
When I broke off her arm.

My mommy looked at Sissy,
She slowly shook her head.
"If someone treated you like this,
I think that you'd be dead."

But I looked up and smiled.
I know I would not care.
In fact, I'd like to go outside,
Without my shoes or underwear.

On Picking Your Nose

I watched Bobby pick his nose,
Then he wiped it on his clothes.
I don't know if Bobby knows, or not—
When clothes get washed, that turns back to snot.

That snot will float in the washing machine,
And none of Bobby's clothes will get clean.
A good detergent might get out dirt,
But you won't catch me wearing Bobby's shirt!

His mommy can wash his clothes all day,
But she'll never wash that snot away.
And you never know just where it goes,
But I know for sure, it's in Bobby's clothes.

That's why, every time I pick my nose,
I keep my finger away from my clothes.
I've better manners. I'm a whole lot neater.
But my friends all call me, "Booger Eater."

My Goldfish

How do goldfish hold their breath so long?
They must have lungs that are really strong.
On the bottom they don't seem to care.
But they might die if they don't get air.

I don't mind them swimming around,
But I don't want my fish to drown.
There's Mommy, Daddy, and a little daughter.
They need to breathe! I took them out of the water.

I put them on the living room floor.
No need to hold their breath anymore.
Those fish know how much I care.
No one else lets them out for air.

They're all very pretty and make nice pets.
But goldfish are as dumb as anything gets.
I try to feed them, but when I get near,
All my goldfish seem to disappear

WALTER PARKER

Walter Parker

I hate that Walter Parker.
His toes are really fat,
He gets bad grades in school,
And it smells bad where he sat.

I really hate Walter Parker.
His glasses are very nerdy,
He makes disgusting noises,
And his shoes are always dirty.

I hate, hate, hate Walter Parker.
It's the way he parts his hair,
How he zips his zipper,
And the clothes he likes to wear.

Oh, how I hate Walter Parker.
I might even hate his mom.
But what I dislike the most about him,
He didn't invite me to the prom.

My Trip To The Zoo

I went to the zoo. Big deal! Who cares!
They wouldn't let me feed the bears.
AND THAT MADE ME MAD!

At the circus a lion balanced on a ball.
At the zoo, lions did nothing at all.
I WAS DISAPPOINTED!

Then, a little while later,
I tried to go swimming with an alligator.
THEY WOULDN'T LET ME!

I felt bad and wanted to sit,
So I thought I would rest in the tiger pit.
BUT SOMEBODY LOCKED THE CAGE!

So I walked around for a little while,
And wanted to pet the crocodile.
BUT THEY SAID NO!

I ran over to the gorilla house to see,
If some of them wanted to play with me.
BUT THEY COULDN'T!

So what fun is a zoo anyway?
None of the animals are allowed to play.
All you can do is stand and stare,
At the wonderful animals everywhere.

The Baby

Daddy calls me baby,
His precious little joy.
I don't know what precious means,
But I'm not a little boy.

I've done a lot of grown-up things,
And those things were not so hard.
I walked all the way, and back,
To our next-door neighbors yard.

I've almost started reading,
It's easier than it looks.
Because I can read the pictures,
In my brother's comic books.

Please don't call me baby!
It's nothing that I like.
I can almost do my zipper,
And I can already ride my trike.

But still he calls me baby.
Each time he must be told,
"I'm not a little baby.
I'm almost three years old"!

The Shower

I don't know if my sister is still in the shower,
But I know she's been in there for over an hour.
Just how important can her first date be?
I'm her brother. Can't she think about me?

She says that I can wait, and that she doesn't care,
She'll still be awhile because she's doing her hair.
It's been over an hour for the hair on her head!
When she unlocks this door I might already be dead!

OPEN UP! This water in my eye isn't a tear,
And I felt something drip out of my ear.
When will you decide that your hair looks great?
Get out of the bathroom and go on your date!

OPEN UP! You can't stay in there all day.
You'll be responsible if my teeth float away.
Just get out for a minute! Please think about me.
I have to get in there, because I have to -
     USE THE BATHROOM REALLY BAD!

Outside Naked

Little brother's outside naked,
He's not wearing any clothes.
Splashing in a puddle,
With mud between his toes.

He's jumping and he's running,
A happy little guy.
Pushing our red sailboat,
A twinkle in his eye.

He's laughing and he's joyful,
A smile upon his face.
If I were five years younger,
Then I could take his place.

That isn't going to happen,
It's just not meant to be.
He's only twenty-seven,
While I'm already thirty-three.

51

My Mommy's Name

What a stupid question-
"What's my mommy's name?"
My mommy's name is Mommy.
Tommy's mommy is the same.

My mommy's name's just Mommy,
With Tommy, that's not true.
Her name is Tommy's Mommy.
(But he calls her Mommy too)

Sometimes it gets confusing,
Like at the grocery or the mall.
A boy was screaming, "Mommy!"
But I didn't know the boy at all.

I guess my mommy knew him,
Because she said, "Look at that."
I hope you never turn out,
Like that spoiled little brat.

The Pirate

I want to be a pirate,
But it's really very hard.
Mommy says that I'm too little,
For me to leave our yard.

So how can I sail the seven seas,
I'm ten feet away from backyard trees.
And Mommy always thinks I look cute,
When I'm dressed up in a business suit.

So even if my chest gets tattooed and hairy,
I still don't think I would look very scary.
Because all you could see as I walked by,
Is a powder blue shirt with a matching tie.

A business suit needs to stay pressed and clean.
But some of those pirates can be really mean.
I don't think Mommy would take it too well,
If someone put fish guts on my lapel.

I can usually get Mommy to change her mind.
Lots of hugs and kisses work best, I find.
But with clothes she has such great endurance,
So perhaps when I'm older, I'll sell life insurance.

The Remote Control

My sister's been naughty, but bless my soul,
I went and hid the remote control!
Now when she's snotty, bad, or controlling,
All I let her watch is professional bowling.

And I'm really glad that she loves TV.
Because now she has to listen to me.
If she's spiteful, she knows what she's facing,
Two-and-a-half hours of NASCAR racing.

She watched MTV, in little snatches.
But mostly she watched the wrestling matches.
I've been thinking, if she doesn't polish my shoes,
She might end up watching the six o'clock news.

Big sisters are tricky, they're hateful and mean,
And I've got the worst one that's ever been seen.
It's great having the controller. I can do what I like.
But I have to return it, because she's hidden my bike.

High Heel Shoes

I like Mommy's shoes,
The ones with high heels.
I've tried them on once
And I like how it feels.

When this girl gets older
It will be all that she wears.
But first I need practice
Going up and down stairs.

Daddy claims he likes them,
I'm not sure that it's true.
If he really liked them
He'd be wearing some too.

Of my two parents,
Mommy is the smaller.
I'll bet she wears them
To help her look taller.

I won't care if I'm short or tall
It won't matter to me at all.
If I'm a doctor, or report the news,
All I am wearing are high heel shoes.

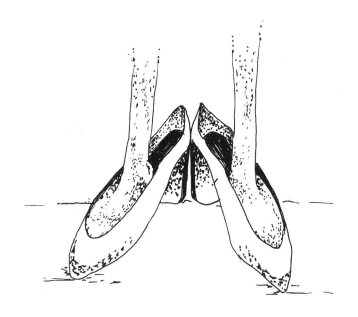

The Married Goldfish

I think my older brother lied.
I'll bet one of my goldfish died.
He wouldn't get married
    and move away.
He doesn't even
    go outside to play.

He's never really
    gone very far,
He always stays
    in the goldfish jar.
That little goldfish
    was happy with his life.
So why would he go
    and look for a wife?

Perhaps he died while I was in school.
Does my brother think I'm such a fool?
Doesn't he realize I'm already three?
He shouldn't keep things away from me.

I think he didn't want me to be sad.
So I went to get the truth from dad.
Now that we talked, I feel much better.
He said my goldfish will write me a letter.

Milk

My brother said milk comes from a cow.
I think he's started a big lie now
Milk doesn't come from somewhere that drastic
It comes from bottles that are made of plastic.

My smarty-pants brother can't tell me how,
They get those bottles out of that cow.
Those bottles are printed in blue and white.
And there is no cow that can read and write.

I stood close to a cow for almost an hour,
Its body was warm, so the milk would go sour.
I guess my brother will tell me a new lie now.
He'll say milk comes from a "refrigerated" cow.

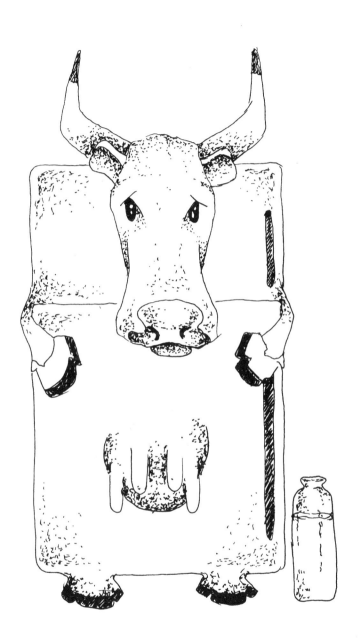

59

I Am Great

There is no hippopotamus who can spell as well as me;
And I can read much better than any ape in any tree.
I hardly ever practice, I usually do it just for fun,
But there isn't any caterpillar, who I can not out-run.

And of all the fish now swimming in the sea,
Not a single one can type as well as me.
Against all the lions in Africa, I would do the best,
If we all had to take my 4th grade history test.

I'm meaner than a teddy bear, faster than a snail.
When it comes to size, I'm much smaller than a whale.
I'm smarter than a rock, and much stronger than an ant.
I can sing a ton of songs, that I know an elm tree can't.

I'm taller than a cat. I speak better than a bear.
When compared to a garden worm, I have a lot more hair.
There isn't any puppy dog between here and Timbuktu,
Who can do the mathematics that I have learned to do.

Not even the birds, or the lemming with all of his buddies,
Could read my language arts book, or the one on social studies.
I'm blessed with skill and knowledge; so it's a mystery to me
That the last six weeks in school, my report card was a "D"!

Pockets

Why do they make pockets so small?
They don't hold very much at all.
Do you know what I have in mine so far?
A frog, a turtle, and a bug in a jar.

A quarter, a penny, three nickels and a dime,
Along with a cap gun that's really not mine.
I have a broken pencil, a ruler and candy.
And a large ball of string, that might come in handy.

I have more stuff, so what should I do?
I've got a spoon and a pocket-knife too.
Six rocks, four marbles, and a large rubber band,
Baseball cards, football cards, and a bag of sand.

My magnet, the compass, a paper clip chain,
A wrench, a socket, and a plug for a drain.
I've got a lizard and this used bottle rocket.
But I think it can fit in my other pocket

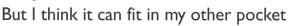

The Lion And The Zebra

The lion and the zebra got married,
And the wedding turned out fine.
But they weren't married very long—
Only until dinnertime.

Aunt Sarah's Baby

You won't believe what Aunt Sarah did.
She went and swallowed a little kid!
It's not a lie! I'm telling the truth.
I touched her tummy, and I felt the proof.

The child she swallowed was not that little.
Aunt Sarah's big, and she's round in the middle.
She seems happy. Even proud of what she did,
But I'd be punished if I swallowed that kid.

I don't know if it's a girl or a boy
But I think she should swallow a toy.
It's probably dark and lonely down there.
The poor kid might want a teddy bear.

Women like her are a dangerous sort,
I bet they think it's some kind of sport.
I'm staying away from all the ladies I see,
I don't want one of them swallowing me.

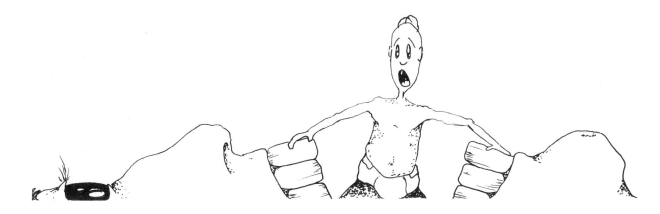

If I Were An Animal

If I were an animal
I know what I'd be.
Nothing unusual,
Just an ape in a tree.

But apes get cold,
And rained on, as well.
I'd still be an ape.
But I'd have a shell.

Then, if it rained,
Or got cold at night,
I'd crawl in my shell
And sleep real tight.

I'd be high in a tree.
See lots of great things.
Make friends with the birds,
So I'd need to have wings.

But I've never flown,
I can't do it that well.
Flying is dangerous.
What if I fell?

If I fell on the land
I could walk over hills.
But if I fell in the ocean
I know I'd need gills.

Then I could breathe.
But one thing more,
I'd still need fins
To swim to shore.

So that is exactly
What I want to be.
Nothing unusual
Just an ape in a tree.

No Underwear

Oh my gosh! I do declare!
I forgot to put on underwear!
The playground is where I want to go,
But if I do my rear will show.

Hopscotch is what I want to play
But I'll have to pass that up today.
I like the slide, but you know what?
Kids would laugh if they saw my butt.

I'm missing the fun and it's not fair.
I tried to get some underwear.
I phoned my mom, but I can't reach her.
I can't leave class, because I'm the teacher.

Right Field

I'm standing out here in right field,
I shouldn't be out here at all.
Samantha's a left-handed batter,
And that girl can murder the ball!

Who put so much sky in right field?
The big leagues look just the same.
There's way too much sky in right field,
This is only a Little League game.

But Samantha has blasted a good one,
And it's somewhere up there in the sky.
I know it's coming to right field,
And I think that I'm going to cry.

I hate her! I hate her! I hate her!
Why did she hit it to me?
We've got a shortstop, a pitcher, a catcher,
Why not to one of those three?

It's way up there in right field,
You can't even see the ball.
It'll probably get down here tomorrow.
That's if it ever gets down here at all.

Mommy and Daddy are screaming.
Their trust is both loyal and pure.
In their hearts, they think I will catch it.
At best, I can say, "I'm not sure."

Her parents should be put into jail,
Letting a little blonde girl use a bat!
She's hit it so high I can't see it.
Perhaps, if I took off my hat.

Wait! I think I can see it!
A small, dark speck in the sky.
And I'm the kid who must catch it.
Baseball history's most difficult fly.

No one in this league's ever caught one,
A rocket from that small slugger's bat.
I reached out my glove; and I missed it,
But the ball somehow fell in my hat!

"OUT!" Thumbs the ump and she's crying.
Her life, now won't be the same.
As for me, I'm a Little League hero!
Gosh, I love playing this game!

Things I've Done

I've done a lot of things
My parents don't know I've done.
I've played with nuclear weapons
And traveled pass the sun.

I've been to a foreign country
And I've driven fancy cars.
Once when they were at dinner,
I took a trip to Mars.

I killed a fire-breathing dragon.
He was evil and very mean.
I've even been under water
And driven a submarine.

I've flown supersonic fighters,
Saved the world once or twice.
I've been to Monte Carlo
Where they let me roll the dice.

Sometimes I'm in disguise,
I use many different names.
I'm being totally honest
I'm good at video games.

Food I Will Not Eat

There are many things I will not eat,
Like toads and snails and puppy feet.
If you made soup, from a dinosaur bone,
I may come to dinner, but you'd eat it alone.

You can fix it with love, serve it with a smile,
But I'd say "no thanks" to baked crocodile.
And I won't eat ants, cockroaches, or worms,
They don't look tasty and might have germs.

It could be the sweetest, best tasting meat,
If you cooked Rudolph, I just would not eat.
Please don't feed me mothballs, spiders, or fleas,
And I won't eat the needles, of evergreen trees.

I can list many other things I will not try,
Kitty litter, toilet paper, and octopus eye.
And please don't cook this again. It won't be missed.
I just added broccoli to the top of the list.

My Mother Is Cooking Liver

My mother's cooking liver.
So I think I'll run away.
No one in this house,
Was nice to me today.

It all started with my older brother.
And the sneaky thing he told our mother;
He told a lie that was evil and black.
There was no problem. Until he hit me back.

As for my stuck-up teenage sister,
My iguana likes her, and so he kissed her.
But she screamed till the whole house shook.
Now he's hiding and she wouldn't help look.

Even the baby is upset and crying.
Sure, I did it. There's no sense in lying.
But he hit my toy with a red plastic bat,
It could have broken, so I gave him the cat.

But now I'm in my room,
I have to stay here all day.
My mother's cooking liver,
So I might run away.

Life

A duck that stands upon the shore
Will never learn to swim.
A robin doesn't learn to fly
By clinging to a limb.

A batter doesn't get a hit
By waiting for a walk.
You will never learn to sing
If you're afraid to talk.

Life puts us all on center stage,
Some are ready and some are not.
Remember when your turn comes up
To give it all you've got.

Don't ever be afraid of life.
Do your best at every task.
And treat each person fairly,
That's all that life can ask.

The Capital Letter

today i learned to write much better,
i learned about the capital letter.
small always used to be too small,
but a capital letter makes SMALL, tall.

ANd anOTheR GooD THing About a CAPITAL letter:
if yoU USE thEm riGHt, the WORDs LooK BEttER.
the seCOND GREat thing, I THink i'VE founD,
USING THEM or not, iT DOESN'T change the sound.

So elephant sounds like ELEPHANT, without changing at all.
Except one looks BIG, and the other looks small..
so this ANT is BIG, and this ANT is MEAN,
but this ant is little. he can hardly be seen.

capital letters don't change what you write,
But they put WRITING, in a wHoLe NeW LigHt!
LeTTerS LoOk better WheN YoU MaKe Them MiX
But I always write my age as a CAPITAL 6.

Daddy's Truck

I'm going to drive my daddy's truck
Just as fast as it can go.
Then I'll roll the windows down
And blast the radio.

I'm not going to stop at red lights.
I'll drive on the railroad track.
All my friends will ride with me
In the truck bed in the back.

I'll put a sign on the bumper.
A sticker that says "NO FEAR".
Then I'll cruise around this town
In the highest, fastest gear.

Daddy said that I could do it.
It was an easy thing to settle.
The only thing I have to do.
Grow enough to reach the pedal.

If You Spoke Monkey

If you spoke monkey
And you went to the zoo,
Would a lion or tiger
Want to chat with you?

If you were in the woods
And you went for a walk,
Would the bear and deer
Understand your talk?

And what would happen
If you spoke to the birds?
Would they fly away,
Or heed your words?

If you took a stroll
Upon the beach,
Would the crab and turtle
Understand your speech?

If you spoke monkey
When you went to church.

Your parents would tell you to "Be Quiet"!

I Dressed Myself For School

Mommy got sick when the weather turned cool,
So I have to dress myself for school.
I'm wearing my purple polka-dot hat,
And I'm taking along my baseball bat.

My favorite socks are blue and red,
But there's just one under my bed.
I don't know exactly what I should do.
I guess I'll wear a yellow one too.

I have lots of dresses that are really cute.
But I chose the bottom of my bathing suit.
I can't wear the top because it's too chilly.
And the other kids might think I look silly.

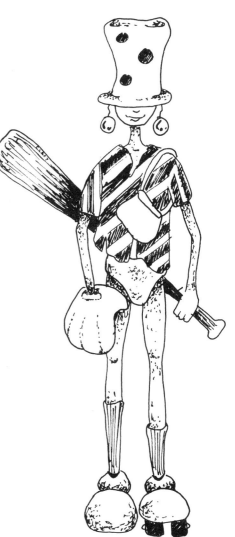

Rhinestone earrings add a special touch.
And I'm wearing lipstick, but not too much.
Mommy's blue eye shadow is what I'll wear,
It matches the glitter I put in my hair.

My favorite blouse is dirty and split,
But it goes well with this catcher's mitt.
I can't find one shoe, and it's getting late,
So on the other foot, it's a roller skate.

I'd like to show Mommy and watch her fuss.
But outside waiting is the school bus.
This afternoon she'll get a big surprise,
I bet Mommy won't believe her eyes!

The Purple Cow

I used to have a purple cow,
She ate no grass at all.
Instead of standing in a field,
She'd bounce a yellow ball.

Sometimes her milk was lemon,
Sometimes her milk was lime.
But I want to have a normal cow,
So I sold her for a dime.

The Greatest Me

I am the greatest me,
That ever was alive.
I've been quite sure of this,
Since I was almost five.

Because no one else but me,
Knows exactly what I think,
And when my eyes get dry,
I'm the one who makes me blink.

I'm the only person
Who can move my toes and feet
So I'm the only one,
Who can make my day complete.

And if I'm the greatest me,
Then it surely must be true,
Of all the people in the world,
You are the greatest you!

Susan Did It

Susan is a magical girl
With a pretty, turned-up nose.
Her feet are so very tiny,
She flosses between her toes.

Susan has delicate fingers,
They are long and very thin.
And if she touches you with one,
It could poke you like a pin.

Her teeth are just like diamonds,
They sparkle in the light.
She wears them as a necklace,
When she goes to bed at night.

Her ears are very pretty,
Just as pretty as you please.
Studded with golden earrings,
That hang down to her knees.

Miss Susan wears silver slippers,
With a long white flowing dress.
And I think that she snuck in here,
That's why my room's a mess.

The Watermelon Seed

My older brother swallowed a watermelon seed.
His tummy's gonna pop, his head is gonna bleed.
He says there's no way for him to get hurt,
Because he ate the seed, but not any dirt.

While that may be true, if he were wiser,
He'd know that poop is a fertilizer.
Fertilizer makes things grow really fast,
I kind of doubt if my brother will last.

We usually get along pretty well,
So I might miss him. You never can tell.
But the good thing is, since we're both boys,
When he blows up, I get to keep his toys.

My Bad Brother

DO YOU KNOW WHAT MY BROTHER DID!

He started a fire.
He called me a liar.
Pinned a clothespin on the kitty's tail.
He threw trash in the yard,
Closed the screen door too hard.
Ripped up all of the morning mail.
He didn't make his bed,
And the dog's not been fed.
He put our hamster in the microwave.
Didn't comb his hair.
Knocked over a chair.
Spent the money I was trying to save.
The toilet's not flushed,
His teeth ain't been brushed.
He put glue in the shampoo jar.
Put a frog down my shirt,
Pinched my nose till it hurt.
He put paint on our daddy's car.
And he still isn't through,
He'll do other things too.

BUT AT LEAST HE'S BEING GOOD TODAY!

Wild Animals

You will never see a rhinoceros miss,
Give her rhinoceros mate a kiss.
She might poke him right in the eye,
Then you'd see both rhinoceros cry.

Some advice given by a mommy polar bear,
"Don't sit too long on your potty chair."
They live in the arctic I've been told,
And a potty chair can get really cold.

If twins are born to a hippopotamus,
She can't do things like the rest of us.
Each little hippo needs his own separate bib,
And they both can't sleep in the same tiny crib.

Cleats are not part of an elephant's baseball clothes,
Because if he ran too fast he might step on his nose.
And even though he is strong and fat,
He could not take his turn at bat.

I could tell you other things too,
None are lies, they would all be true.
There's much more information I can give,
Because I know how wild things live.

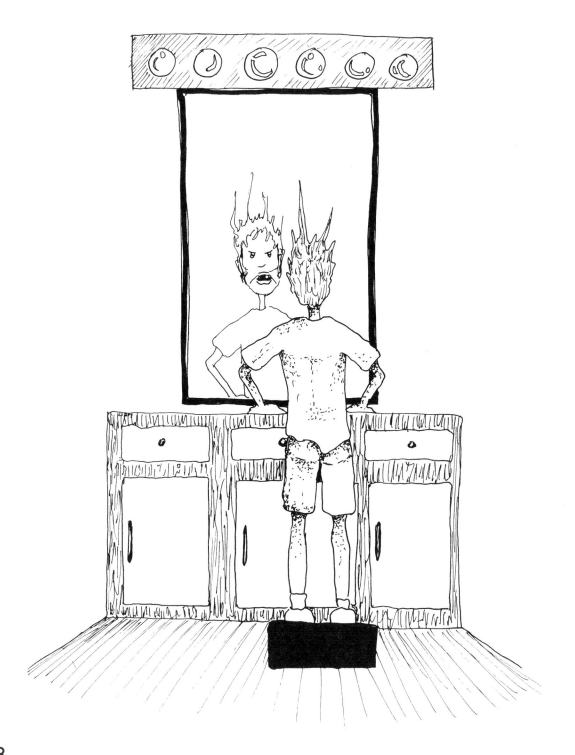

The Ugly Little Boy

That's the ugliest little boy,
I think I've ever seen.
His cheeks are red and puffy,
His eyes are small and mean.

His lower lip is swollen,
He's missing two front teeth.
Is that his chin I'm looking at,
Or a pound of chopped up beef?

He didn't comb his hair,
It sticks out from his head.
I'm sure he didn't wash himself,
When he climbed out of his bed.

His clothes are ripped and wrinkled,
He's got dirt behind his ears.
And they're so full of earwax,
I doubt if he even hears.

It's just a joke. I'm kidding.
Don't believe a word you hear.
How could I not realize,
That I was looking in a mirror.

Climbing

I'm the best climber upper,
That, no one can debate.
You'd never find one better,
In this entire state.

I've climbed up on a rocking horse,
I've climbed our neighbor's fence.
But the neighbor told my mommy,
So I haven't climbed it since.

I've climbed up on my father's chair,
When Daddy was not at home.
I've climbed up on the bathroom sink,
So that I could reach the comb.

Now I've climbed the highest tree.
I can see for miles around.
I sure hope someone rescues me.
I have trouble climbing down.

My Family

We all live in one big family,
But it's confusing to a girl like me.
Relationships are hard to define,
I've been trying to sort out mine.
I call my father Daddy,
Mommy calls him Daddy too.
Yet, when I say that he's her daddy,
She tells me that it's not true.
(I suspect her daddy's Grandpa
Because she calls him Daddy too.)
My brother's sister Sara,
Well, she's my sister too.
But talking about my mommy's sister,
That same rule don't hold true.
I called my mommy's sister, "Sister,"
But they told me that I can't.
They said when I refer to her,
I'm supposed to call her, "Aunt".
But my father has a sister,
So what am I to do?
She's not my mother's sister,
Do I call her "Aunty" too?
My brother is my other brother's brother,
But for me, that can't apply,
They say that I'm their sister,
So I guess that's the reason why.
And my father has a sister-in-law,
I don't know how that can be,
Maybe I'm too young for law,
I only just turned three.

But there is one thing I'm sure of,
One thing that will always be:
I will always love my family,
And I know they all love me.

The Sleeping Cat

My cat was asleep beneath a tree,
When she got stung by a yellow bee.
She cried and screamed and danced around,
She even clawed our blue-tic hound.

I thought that cat had met its end,
She and Blue were never friend.
I was sure he'd rip out Kitty's throat,
But instead he went and bit the goat.

The goat just stood in total surprise,
But a fire quickly grew in his eyes.
I knew he'd kill that dog, of course,
But he decided to butt the horse.

A horse won't fight, it will usually flee.
But he got so mad, that he kicked me.
I'd like to scream and shout and weep.
But I can't make noise, the cat's asleep.

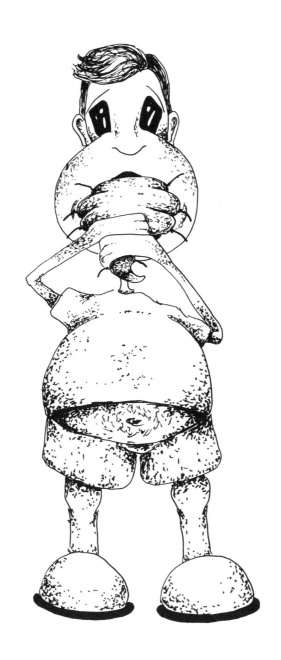

On Eating Bugs

I ain't never gonna eat another bug again.
But he was wiggling in my clothes,
And he crawled right between my toes.
So I ate him.

But I ain't never gonna eat another bug again.
Not even if he tickles me on my arm,
Not even if I think he'll do me harm.
I just won't eat him.

Nope, I ain't never gonna eat another bug again.
He can be green, and just as pretty as he wishes,
He can have long legs, he can even look delicious.
I will not eat him!

No I ain't never gonna eat another bug again.
That last time, I was a little bit too hasty,
Those big fat brown ones, they're just not tasty.
And I ain't never gonna eat another bug again.

My Body

I don't think God was being too fair,
I didn't get enough legs or hair.
A spider has eight, a horse has four,
I could have used just a few more.

If my whole body were covered with hair,
I'd never wear a coat. No one would care.
The extra legs would help me run faster,
If Mommy chased me, I could run right past her.

A monkey spends all day swinging by his tail
He doesn't worry if he'll pass or fail.
Cows spend their time munching on grass.
They never listen to a teacher in class.

Little baby owls can stay up all night.
Their moms never worry if they read or write.
My mommy, worries about my grades, of course,
Doesn't she know?

I PLAN TO BE A HORSE!

Uncle Harold

Uncle Harold is a college professor.
A nice old man, but a terrible dresser.
He has a nose that is big and wide.
With lots of hair that grows inside.

If he's so smart, and so well read,
Can't he grow some hair on his head?
Perhaps if one studies for too many years,
They like having hair grow inside their ears.

He has tons of knowledge inside that head,
It's pushed on his face till his nose turned red.
And all that knowledge has to be recalled.
I guess it's easier if your head is bald.

Uncle Harold never worries about looks.
He only cares about what's inside his books.
I was worried it would happen to me.
So isn't it lucky, that I made this "D".

Mr. McCullah's Magical Zoo

Have you been to Mr. McCullah's magical zoo?
The entrance fee is just a dollar or two.
You won't believe the things that he's got.
But I've been there, and seen them, believe it or not.

First there's an elephant, half white and half black,
With a trunk in the front and a trunk in the back.
But that's not the thing that's amazing at all.
This elephant is exceedingly small.

He's kept on the head of a pin, in a jar.
And none of the customers have seen him so far.
So I looked and I stared, because my eyes are keen,
But that magical elephant just couldn't be seen.

The next thing Mr. McCullah put on display,
Was a flying horse which he bought in Bombay.
He shouted and pointed as the steed flew by.
I never knew a horse could fly that high.

Now I've ridden horses, none of them wild.
I knew a cowboy when I was a child.
But I'd never ride that horse, I'd be afraid to fall.
He was up there so high, I never saw him at all.

For just six dollars more you could stay where you sat.
Because he had a gorilla that looked like a cat.
I wondered if Mr. McCullah might be a cheat.
But I paid my six dollars and I stayed in my seat.

Out came an animal that I'm sure looked like a cat.
He had a long furry tail, and was fluffy and fat.
His whiskers were long, and he had claws on his feet.
So as a test, I gave him a banana to eat.

I don't know what caused it, and I don't know how,
But he looked at the banana, and he said, "Meow!"
I've read about gorillas. I know a thing or two.
There are many tricks that you can teach them to do.

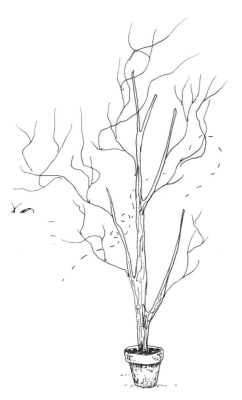

Sit up. Roll over. Balance a ball on their brow.
But you can't teach a gorilla to say meow.
Yet, this gorilla said it! So it must be true!
Mr. McCullah really does have a magical zoo!

So for another six dollars, you know what you'd see?
A large scaly dragon! That looks just like a tree!
And I would have done it, would have paid in a flash,
But seeing the gorilla took the last of my cash.

But I'll tell you for certain, I know what I'll do.
Next time in the neighborhood I'll revisit that zoo.
It's known as Mr. McChullah's Magical Zoo.
If you'd like to come with me, you can visit it too.

Smoking

I smoked my first cigar today.
I only smoked it about half way.
Even then, before I was through,
It hurt my head, and my tummy too.

It was big, and round, and brown,
It flipped my insides up-side-down.
But I kept puffing (which was not too wise)
Because pretty soon, it hurt my eyes.

I got dizzy; didn't feel well,
I didn't even like the smell.
Smoke was blowing up my nose,
I dropped hot ashes on my clothes.

My friend said smoking looks so cool.
But I really feel like a fool.
Next time, candy or gum will be my pick,
And I won't be sitting here - green and sick.

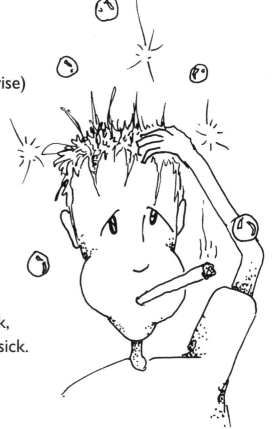

The Not Too Funny Section

*Some of the poems that follow are
about things that happened as far back
as the 1960s (1943 for "The Sailor").
You may want to read this section with
an adult or a "really old" person.*

My Mother Is Being Unfair

The sun is up and shining,
The sky is blue and fair.
Mommy says that I must stay here,
That I'm not going anywhere.

Why can't she let me ride my bike,
It's only a mile or two.
I promise that I'd be right back,
The moment I was through.

I could go out walking,
It's such a lovely day.
I could find some brand new friends,
And we could stay outside and play.

Looking out the window,
There's a grassy park, I see.
With lots of other little kids,
Who want to play with me.

I don't think she is being fair,
The day is so bright and pretty.
I don't like staying in this hotel,
And I don't like New York City!

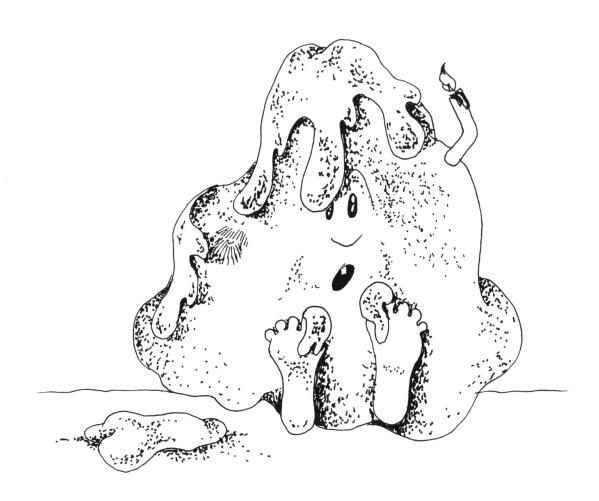

Mitch's Birthday

My parents gave my brother a birthday cake,
Personally, I think it was a big mistake.
I'm glad the party wasn't formal dress.
My little brother made a terrible mess.

He didn't use a fork or silverware,
He threw cake and frosting everywhere.
I doubt he even heard the birthday cheers,
With all that cake stuffed inside his ears.

His bib could not protect his clothes,
He even blew frosting from his nose.
He rubbed big gobs on his hair and cheeks.
I think he'll be a mess for weeks.

We were all laughing, having a good time,
While Mitch turned himself into birthday slime.
My parents are smart and shouldn't need to be told,
You don't give a birthday cake, to a one-year-old.

My Summer Vacation

I wish summer would come.
You know what I'm going to do?
I'm going to visit the Kalama Zoo.

They don't have a lion,
No tigers, no bear.
But they have lots of Kalama's there.

I asked my brother,
And if he hasn't lied,
They're soft and furry, and fun to ride.

They like little boys,
And little girls too.
I've been told they play games with you.

They love Monopoly,
And Hide-and-Go-Seek.
When it's his turn to count, a Kalama won't peek.

I know I'll love the Kalama Zoo,
The rest of summer won't be much fun.
I'm visiting my grandparents in Michigan.

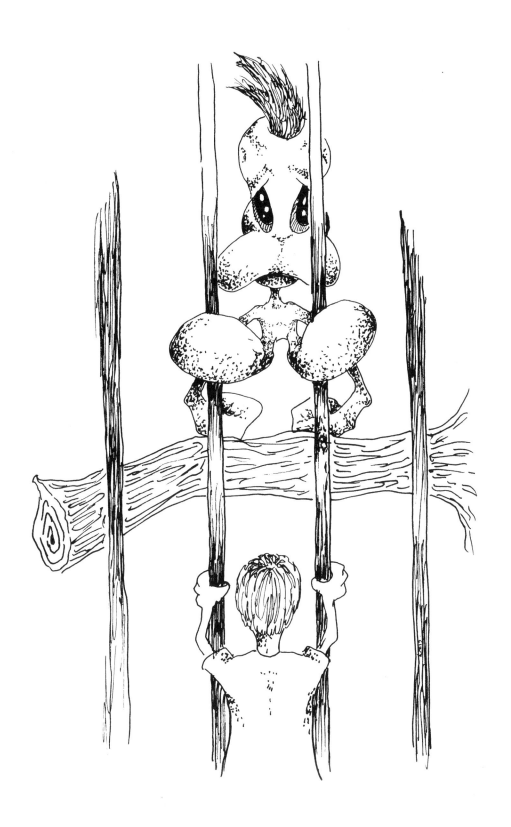

109

The Sailor

My father died upon the sea
Ten thousand miles away from me.
A naval engagement near Japan,
My father was a Navy man.

I miss his touch, I miss his face,
But I don't lament his resting place.
He now sleeps upon the ocean floor
Some hundred miles from the shore.

I walk the beach. I touch a wave.
I stand within my father's grave.
He gave his life protecting me.
Men like him have kept us free.

A Soldier's Prayer

God doesn't look at the uniform,
But He looks at the man within.
The lowly private, or a general,
It's all the same to Him.

Never was there a battle fought,
Where good men have not died.
Where angels have taken to heaven,
Brave soldiers from either side.

Yet we must fight our nation's battles,
Go on till our last breath.
But never rejoice at killing,
And never rejoice in death.

So if you ever kill a soldier,
Don't cheer at his passing away.
But pray he was noble and honest,
You may meet him in heaven one day.

My Athletic Daddy

Daddy told me all about his athletic fame.
He's never dropped a pass in a Rose Bowl game.
And when it comes to hockey, he plays it well,
He's never been scored on in the NHL.

I've never seen him play basketball.
So he's had a pretty long lay-off.
But he's never missed a foul shot,
In a NBA playoff.

Someday I hope to be as good.
I'm his son. I carry his name.
He say's he's never struck out,
In a World Series Game.

And I learned just the other night,
He's never lost an Olympic fight.
I find it amazing that he's done all that,
Daddy's very short, and he's also fat.

A Future Engineer

Why are wheels on the bottom,
And why is the roof on top?
Wheels can keep things moving,
But a roof can make them stop.

If I roll my Barbie car
Across the kitchen floor,
With the wheels pointing down
The car will hit the kitchen door.

But if I set it on it's roof,
And then I push the car,
It has no trouble stopping,
It isn't going very far.

And I know what this tells me;
I think I've found the proof,
That cars would stop much better
If the wheels were on the roof.